ANTI-BULLYING BASICS

BULLIED *by Groups*

WORLD BOOK

A Scott Fetzer company
Chicago
worldbook.com

World Book, Inc.
233 North Michigan Avenue
Suite 2000
Chicago, Illinois 60601 U.S.A.

For information about other World Book publications, visit our website at www.worldbook.com or call 1-800-967-5325.

The contents of this book were reviewed by Kari A. Sassu, Ph.D., NCSP, assistant professor, Counseling and School Psychology Department, and coordinator, School Psychology Program, Southern Connecticut State University, New Haven, Connecticut.

Product development: Arcturus Publishing Ltd
Writer: Jen Green
Editor and picture researcher: Nicola Barber
Designer: Ian Winton

Staff

Library of Congress Cataloging-in-Publication Data

Bullied by groups.
    pages cm. -- (Anti-bullying basics)
  Includes index.
  Summary: "A discussion of bullying by groups, what causes bullying, how bullying affects bullies and their targets; contains advice and useful strategies for targets of bullies"-- Provided by publisher.
  ISBN 978-0-7166-2074-7
  1. Bullying--Juvenile literature. 2. Social groups--Juvenile literature. 3. Bullying--Prevention--Juvenile literature.
I. World Book, Inc.
BF637.B85B825 2014
302.34'3--dc23
                 2013024686

World Book's Anti-Bullying Basics   Set ISBN: 978-0-7166-2070-9
Printed in China by PrintWORKS Global Services, Shenzhen, Guangdong
2nd printing January 2015

3 9082 12788 5849

Contents

What Is Bullying?

Bullying is unwanted, deliberately hurtful behavior that is repeated over a period of time. Bullying is often about an imbalance of power—bullies may use their physical strength, popularity, or something they know about another person to harm or control others.

Forms of bullying

Bullying can take many forms, including verbal, physical, social, and cyberbullying (a form of bullying on digital devices).

- Verbal bullying includes name-calling, teasing, inappropriate comments, threats, and abusive comments.
- Physical bullying includes hitting, kicking, spitting, tripping, and stealing or damaging possessions.
- Social bullying includes deliberately excluding someone from social events, spreading rumors about a person, and embarrassing or humiliating someone.
- Cyberbullying includes harassment and abuse via a cell phone, on social media sites, or online.

What bullying is not

Bullying is not:
- single occurrences of rejection, nastiness, or spite
- random acts of aggression
- one-time arguments or disagreements

All of these events can cause unhappiness. While falling out with friends or dealing with occasional disagreements may not be pleasant, they are a normal part of the process of learning and growing up. These occasional "dramas" in everyday life are very different from bullying, which is deliberate and repeated aggressive behavior that is intended to cause harm and unhappiness.

ABOUT THESE BOOKS

This series of books—*Anti-Bullying Basics*—
examines six different aspects of bullying:
bullying by groups, bullying by boys, bullying by
girls, bullying in cyberspace, bullying by friends,
and bullying to "fit in." Each book examines the
causes and effects of a particular type of bullying
and provides support and practical advice for
dealing with bullies. Bullying happens everywhere
in society: It often goes unchecked because of the
fear it creates and because people don't take it
seriously.

Why it's serious

Bullying is serious because it can have a damaging effect on the person being
bullied, on the person doing the bullying, and even on the bystanders who
witness incidents of bullying. Bullying creates a climate of fear, and bystanders
may be anxious that they will be next on the bully's list of targets. The targets,
the people who are being bullied, are more likely to lack self-confidence, have
low self-esteem, have difficulty concentrating, and suffer from depression and
anxiety. People who bully are at greater risk than others of becoming involved
in violence and crime. Bullies also have a higher risk of struggling or failing at
their school studies. Young people who are both bullies and bullied are at the
highest risk of mental health problems later in life. And, both bullies and their
targets may have a more difficult time forming healthy relationships as adults.

Types of Social Groups

A social group is a set of people who share the same interests. It can be great to be part of a group and to know your friends are looking out for you. However, social groups can become involved in bullying. Some form of bullying goes on every day in every school.

Types of social groups

There are many types of social groups. Maybe you call your group of friends your crew or your peeps. Maybe others call your set a clique—a tightly knit group of friends that tends to dress and act the same and that excludes any not in the clique. Whatever you call your set, belonging to a group of friends can give you a sense of well-being. However, in a group it's also quite easy to get caught up in what is going on and do or say something that you wouldn't if you were on your own. This could include being mean to others or bullying. If you are in a group, it's good to be aware of this danger and to hold fast to your sense of what is right.

Being part of a social group can give you a sense of well-being.

ASHAMED OF BEING BULLIED

Jaylah was bullied by a group of girls because of her skin color. When the girls started taunting her or throwing things at her, she would lock herself in a toilet stall and quietly sob. Jaylah felt ashamed of being bullied. Her grades fell, and she started to skip classes. When her mother found out about her problem and told the principal, he held a meeting with the bullies and explained to them they would be suspended from school if the behavior continued. He then informed the bullies' parents about the situation. They soon left Jaylah alone.

Many social groups grow out of shared interests and activities.

Group Identity

Many people enjoy the feeling of belonging that comes from being in a group. A group of friends can help give you a sense of identity—of who you are—that may make you feel more confident. However, in some groups, this sense of belonging involves defining people who are not in the group as "different," and this can often lead to bullying.

Being in the group

Many cliques and clubs have a group "look." Members wear similar clothes and jewelry. They may share similar tastes in music, fashion, and movies, and like doing the same things.

Defining others as different

Being in a social group can make you feel supported. It's great to know your friends are there for you through good times and bad. But in some sets, the entire group identity is based on seeing others as different. These differences may be based on gender, age, race, religious beliefs, sexual preference, class, or wealth. No matter how these differences are defined, they can potentially lead to bullying.

Members of school bands often form social groups around their interest in music.

BULLYING Q & A

How do I get accepted?

Q. There is a large group of popular kids in my high school. I wish I could get in with them. How can I get them to accept me as one of the group?

....

A. Are you so sure you even want that? High school is the most important thing in your life now. But, in a few years, you will have moved on and you may never see people from your high school again. What is it that seems so appealing about this group? Is the group filled with people who discuss interesting books and movies? With people who volunteer their time at a homeless shelter? Do the people in this group listen to great music? Try to imagine what sorts of things you wish you did. Volunteer at a shelter. Begin a book club with your current friends. Do things to enrich your life, and find friends who will do them with you. You'll be happier now and have a happier future.

Safety in Numbers?

Being a member of a social group can make you feel as if you are a member of a protective family. You may feel stronger and more confident with your friends around you. But belonging to some types of groups may not be as safe as you think.

Protection

Groups provide strength in numbers. You may feel that this strength will protect you against bullying.

Is it safe?

Being in a group may make you feel safe, but you may have developed a false sense of security. Teens in groups are more likely to be involved in fights. Avoid joining a social group made up of aggressive or mean members. You want the society of a group of like-minded friends, not a group that will involve you in conflicts and problems. Being the bully can be as harmful, at times, as being bullied.

BULLYING Q & A

Should I carry a weapon?

Q. I was recently bullied by a group of kids at school. One of the boys pulled a knife and threatened me with it. Now, I feel afraid at school. Should I get a knife too?

....

A. Carrying a knife to school is a terrible idea. For one thing, if the knife is taken away from you in a fight, it can then be turned on you. A knife won't make you safer, in fact quite the opposite: It will put you in greater danger.

Weapons and school

Weapons should never be brought to school. Nearly all schools have policies that forbid students to bring weapons to school. Students can be suspended or expelled from school for having a weapon on school grounds.

If you see that any student has a weapon at school, find the nearest teacher, counselor, or administrator and tell them immediately. This is a serious issue and you should always report it.

....

Joining the Club

Running with a group of friends can be fun. But some groups and clubs allow you to join only if you pass an *initiation* (joining ceremony) that can involve abuse or humiliation. Some of these initiations are really group bullying under a different name.

Hazing and initiation

In the United States and Canada, entry into school and college social clubs, such as fraternities, sororities, societies, and even getting into marching bands, may involve violent or abusive initiations called "hazing." Anyone wishing to join has to prove him- or herself by passing a test or trial. This could involve anything from reciting the club rules from memory to being bullied, beaten, or having to bully someone else. Members have been seriously hurt or even killed in hazing ceremonies that have gotten out of hand.

If you join a group and discover it involves hazing, it is important to refuse to participate in activities that will hurt you or others and to report these activities. You should report any hazing problems to a school administrator.

Such college organizations as marching bands may have hazing initiations for joining members. In 2011, a drum major at Florida A&M University collapsed and died after a hazing incident, causing the school to closely examine the culture of the band. Hazing was subsequently outlawed by the university.

Are they really so cool?

From the outside, teen clubs and societies can seem really hip and cool, especially if most members are a little older than you are. However, once in, many members discover that life in the group is less exciting and glamorous than it seemed from the outside.

HAZING HORROR

Pete was excited to join a fraternity during his freshman year at college. But his initiation involved being kicked and beaten, having to eat bizarre combinations of food, and being publicly humiliated. When he tried to stand up for himself, he was threatened and bullied. He refused to join the fraternity.

....

Pete has now graduated and works as a volunteer discussing the dangers of hazing. Hazing is illegal on many campuses and in some U.S. states. Pete's organization works to make hazing illegal everywhere in the United States.

Starting college should be a positive experience for everyone.

Group Bullying

Many social groups are harmless and great fun to be in. Other sets develop a *culture* (the behaviors and beliefs of a group) that includes bullying. In these groups, it becomes normal for members to bully or abuse people who are outside the group. The group gains a reputation for being tough and mean.

Deliberate exclusion from a group can be a form of bullying.

Group bullying can take many different forms.

• **Physical bullying**

  may involve pushing people, punching, kicking, pinching, or hair-pulling; burning people with cigarettes; cutting them with knives; or spitting on them. It can also include damaging someone's things, or spoiling their homework assignments.

  ....

• **Verbal bullying**

  may involve calling people hurtful names, or verbally threatening them with physical harm.

  ....

• **Cyberbullying**

  may involve the use of e-mails, cell phones, websites, or social networking sites to spread threats, slurs, or rumors about a person.

  ....

• **Relational bullying**

  (also called relational aggression) may involve harm or threats to harm a target's relationships or social status. A group may ignore you and not allow you to join in their activities. Or, they might try to take away your friends.

  ....

BULLYING Q & A

Teasing or bullying?

Q. A clique of girls in my class is being really mean to me. They make fun of the way I look and talk, and they call me names. Now they have started threatening me. No one has actually touched me, but I feel really upset and frightened. Am I being bullied?

....

A. You are definitely being bullied. Calling people names can hurt just as much as physical bullying, and threats can be really scary. No one should have to put up with being bullied. The best thing would be to tell a trusted adult, such as a teacher or counselor at your school, who can put a stop to the bullying.

Bullying by cell phone is a
growing problem.

Who Gets Bullied?

Groups commonly target people outside their circle of friends. There are times, though, when they turn on their own members. So even if you are part of the group, you may live with the uneasy feeling that you could be the next target.

When bullies target people they consider "different," people of others religions are sometimes bullied.

Why pick on me?

Groups that bully usually pick on anyone whom they define as different. They may focus on physical features such as a person's size or weight. Teens have been bullied because they are shorter or taller than average, because of their hair color, clothes, or because they wear glasses. Someone might be bullied because they have a scar, acne, or a speech problem. The opposite can also be true: Sometimes people are bullied because they are considered good-looking or find it easy to get good grades.

Sometimes, however, a person can become a target of a group even if he or she is a member of that group. The target may be threatened that she will no longer be a part of the group if she refuses to do something the group wants, perhaps. This type of bullying within the group is particularly common among pre-adolescent girls.

Choosing to see difference

Bullying groups also target people whom they define as different concerning more meaningful traits. People may be bullied because of their race, religion, or culture; because they have special needs; or because they define themselves as gay. If a group is into bullying, however, they may not choose someone because of a meaningful trait. They often focus on any tiny difference as an excuse, singling out people who are shy, quiet, new in school, or who have few friends to protect them. Bullies will pick on anyone they think they can get away with bullying.

BULLIED FOR BEING GAY

Ben was 13 years old when he came out to a friend about his sexual preference. He confided to a friend that he was gay; but that friend told his best friend, and soon word got around the whole school. Soon after, text messages were sent linking Ben's name with a teacher and implying they were involved sexually. Links to pornography sites appeared on Ben's Facebook page. Then the violence started. The group of bullies giving Ben a problem began beating him up at school. In the end, Ben had to tell his dad, who spoke to the principal. After the school launched a campaign to combat bullies targeting gay students, things slowly improved. In high school, Ben felt alone and defenseless, especially when he was bullied. When he graduated from high school and entered college, however, he found a large group of supportive friends.

Bullying and the Disabled

People who are disabled—especially people who are developmentally disabled—often have a more difficult time at school than their nondisabled peers. They hardly need people to bully them and make their time at school even more difficult. Nevertheless, one study showed that 60 percent of students with disabilities stated they had been bullied, compared to about 30 percent of nondisabled students.

Disabled kids most likely to be bullied

Children with developmental disabilities are more likely to be bullied than those with physical disabilities. Children with autism spectrum disorders (ASD) are often bullied by other children. ASD children can be socially awkward and can have difficulties communicating and relating to others. The more high-functioning an ASD child is, the more likely that child is to be bullied, as they are less likely to be in special-education classes and are more likely to be exposed to bullying when in mainstream classes.

If you are bullying a child in your class who to you seems "strange" or "different," it is possible you may be bullying someone whose brain is wired to work differently than yours. The child who has ASD has no more choice in the matter than you do about your eye color. And, that child is probably far less able to defend him- or herself than you are. Instead of teasing a child who is different, try being kind to that child. You may be surprised by how much better you feel about yourself.

School can be a difficult enough place for children with disabilities without having to cope with the additional stress of bullying.

BULLYING Q & A

How can I help?

Q. My child has an autism spectrum disorder. He is being bullied by children in his class. They push him, make fun of the way he talks, and steal his things from him; it has gotten so he no longer wants to go to school. Is there any way I can help him?

A. If a disabled student is being bullied because of that disability, it can be considered harassment. Disabled students who have an Individualized Education Plan (IEP) qualify for the special protections given under U.S. federal law to the disabled. So do students that have a 504 plan—a plan that gives students the right to the necessary accommodations to ensure their academic success. If a school does nothing to prevent a disabled child from being bullied, the U.S. Office for Civil Rights could find that that child is being denied an equal opportunity for an education. This would be a serious problem for a school. Write a letter to your child's school telling them of the problem and your concerns, and request that the school intervene in this situation.

Why Turn to Bullying?

So why do people in social groups turn to bullying? There are many reasons, but the short answer is that bullying behavior makes bullies feel good in some way. Bullies need help to understand the causes and consequences of their actions.

Group members may encourage each other to bully.

Motives behind bullying

Group bullying starts for a variety of reasons. Ringleaders often do it because it makes them feel powerful. They mistake the fear they inspire in others for respect and popularity. In fact, people who go along with a bully because they are frightened of him or her tend not to be true friends. Bullying does not help anyone to become popular, and it can get people into serious trouble.

Sometimes, bullies are jealous of the person they are bullying. They may feel that their target is smarter or more popular than they are. Sometimes a bully is on the receiving end of bullying behavior elsewhere. In this case, bullying behavior may have come to seem natural. If a person is being hurt either physically or mentally, their response may be to take it out on others.

I'm not responsible!

Within a group, members often encourage one another to become bolder and to take part in increasingly extreme behavior. Situations can often get out of control. Another factor in bullying is that people often feel less responsible for their behavior in a group than they would for actions taken when they were alone. And, some bullying is just thoughtlessness. In the heat of the moment, people don't think about the effect their actions are having on others.

BECOMING A BULLY

In middle school, a clique of girls picked on Jodie. She started hanging out with another group of girls who were really tough, and she joined in when they started bullying. It felt good when she realized that her former bullies were afraid of her. The first group of girls didn't pick on her any more. But, she is secretly afraid of her new group of friends. She's paid a steep price to stop people from bullying her.

Bullying to Impress

Showing off and saving face are often major factors in group-bullying situations. The ringleaders are out to prove they're tough. These bullies thrive on having an audience. Bystanders who are less active in the bullying may nevertheless feel they have to go along with it to keep their place in the group. Even bystanders not in the group may be afraid to stand up to the bullies for fear of becoming a target themselves.

Climate of fear

Some people show off by bullying others because they think it will win them friends. In fact, members of your group who are secretly scared of you are not likely to stand by you when you have a problem. The climate of fear in a bullying group does not encourage true friendship.

Standing by while someone is bullied makes you part of the problem.

Going with the flow

In a group situation, things can get out of hand. It's often hard to define exactly when general teasing turns nasty and becomes hurtful bullying directed at a particular person or people.

You may not think of yourself as a bully, but you are partly responsible if you go along with it. You become one of the bullies if you stand by while someone is hurt or ridiculed. The same is true if you pass on mean texts, notes, or gossip; if you join others in ignoring someone; or if you join in the laughter when one person is the focus of all the jokes.

WHEN FRIENDS TURN ON YOU

When Michael was 14, a group of boys with whom he had been friends turned against him. The name-calling and ridicule seemed worse because it came from people he had thought of as friends. One day as he left school, he ran into one of the bullies on his own. Michael waited for the taunting to begin, but the boy said nothing and looked uncomfortable. Michael realized that the bullies were cowards. The bullying only went on when the ringleaders had a group and the backing of the others. Michael resolved not to let his former friends push him around anymore. Every time the group bullied him, he responded with "I don't care what you think about me" and walked away. Eventually, they grew bored with bullying him.

Standing Up to Bullying

Experiencing some form of bullying is very common. School bullying statistics in the United States show that between 15 and 30 percent of U.S. kids are directly affected by bullying. But group bullying can be particularly tough, because it's often harder to stand up to a group than to an individual. Being bullied by an entire group of kids can make you feel quite alone, as if everyone is against you.

Affecting your performance

Young people who are being bullied by a group often feel scared and anxious. Bullying may start to affect their schoolwork or their performance generally, because they find it hard to concentrate. They might be tempted to pretend they are sick, or skip meals, games, or classes to avoid the bullies. A survey by the National Education Association taken decades ago estimated that some 160,000 U.S. kids a day stayed home from school to avoid bullying. Given the age of this survey, that number is probably far higher today.

You are not responsible!

Targets of group bullying often find it hard to admit they are being bullied. They may feel ashamed or embarrassed because they feel that being bullied makes them look weak. They may even feel somehow responsible for what is happening. If they have been physically injured, their impulse might be to make up excuses for the injuries. For some, admitting to bullying may be even worse than the bullying itself. But by not speaking up, or by hiding the effects of bullying, they are covering up for the bullies, and the bullying is unlikely to stop.

Targets of bullying often feel very alone.

BULLYING Q & A

Is it a joke?

Q. Three kids in my class are making my life wretched. They make fun of my culture and family. They make rude comments about how I dress, everything. They don't pick on anyone else. If I get upset it only makes it worse. They say I can't take a joke, and they were only teasing, but I don't find it funny. Am I a bad sport?

A. If you are always the one that gets picked on, then it is bullying. It's horrible to be laughed at by a group. Don't feel bad about yourself—that's just what the bullies want. If ignoring the bullying doesn't work, the best thing is to tell an adult at your school about what is going on.

Effects of Group Bullying

Being bullied by a group can be a very damaging experience. If you are a confident person, you may be able to shrug it off and not let it get to you. However, for many young people who are less confident and more vulnerable, the effects can last for years.

Effects on self-image

Almost all teens who have been bullied experience a drop in self-confidence. Being bullied can easily alter a person's self-image and self-esteem. You may start to feel you are weak and worthless. It can be hard not to let the bullies' comments about you affect how you see yourself.

Eating disorders and self-harm

Some teens who are bullied may skip meals, and some may develop eating disorders. Sometimes teens who are bullied also harm themselves, for example, by cutting themselves. A few consider suicide as the only way to stop the bullying. Suicide is a leading cause of death among young people. Experts cannot track exactly how many suicides result from bullying. A study by Yale University, however, showed that children who were bullied were two to nine times more likely to consider suicide.

You may start to blame yourself for the bullying, but that is exactly what the bullies want. Try to be kind to yourself. Do things you enjoy, eat regular meals, and get enough sleep—all of these things will help you feel better about yourself. Finding a person you trust—preferably an adult—with whom you can share your feelings and thoughts will also be of great help. No one deserves to be bullied or should have to put up with it.

Some teens who are bullied develop eating disorders.

STARTING OVER

Olivia was 14 when a group of girls started picking on her and saying she was fat. Olivia took the bullying to heart. She looked in the mirror and hated what she saw. She began to skip meals and lost a lot of weight, but the bullying went on. She secretly began to cut her arms, legs, and stomach with a razor. This continued for two years. Then one day she caught sight of her poor, abused body in a mirror. She realized she had to stop self-harming. Olivia talked to a guidance counselor at her school, even though it was really hard for her to admit to the problems she was having. The counselor helped her to find a therapist who specialized in the types of problems Olivia was having. It was hard work, but the therapy helped. Olivia changed schools and made new friends who supported her and helped her to like herself again.

Be kind to yourself—find something you really enjoy doing.

Passing on the Bullying

Bullying can become a pattern in some schools and neighborhoods. Many teens who have experienced bullying themselves feel the only way out is to become a bully. This sets up a chain of bullying. The bullying becomes widespread and is accepted as the norm.

Bullying can become a vicious cycle. But if you are bullied, taking it out on someone else by bullying them won't solve your problem.

Bullying chains

Surveys at schools in the United States have found that as many as four out of five students said they had taken part in some form of bullying. Most of these kids said they had also been bullied themselves. In one survey taken in the United Kingdom, nine out of ten girls questioned said they had been bullied, and two out of three said they had been taken part in bullying activities.

It can seem like the only way to stay safe from bullies is to join a crew of bullies yourself. But that won't necessarily stop the bullying, and it could get you in deeper trouble. For example, if you get labeled as a troublemaker, you may be less likely to be believed if you say that you are being bullied.

Breaking the cycle

The alternative is to take a stand against the bullies, either on your own, or better, with the help of your school. If your group of friends starts to bully, put yourself in the target's shoes. You know how bad it feels to be bullied.

FROM BULLIED TO BULLY

Sam's dad called him a wimp and hit him to toughen him up. Sam started taking it out on a schoolmate, Aaron. Bullying Aaron made Sam feel stronger. When his friends joined in on the bullying, Sam went further and started to take Aaron's things. Watching him panic was a laugh.

One day, Aaron wasn't in school. A teacher explained he had tried to kill himself to end the bullying, and he was now in hospital. Sam felt really bad. Eventually he contacted a helpline. The counselor asked him about his home life and Sam told him about his dad. The counselor helped Sam to see he was taking his own hurt out on Aaron. He went to see Aaron and apologized. Sam is talking to a school counselor now to try to improve his own situation.

Bullied by Family

Sometimes, the people bullying you can be members of a group that should be supporting you and helping you. People can be bullied by members of their family—their siblings (brothers and sisters).

How is bullying different from sibling rivalry?

Siblings will often fight over a toy, a game, or over who gets to sit where. This fighting and competition between brothers and sisters is known as *sibling rivalry*. But if one sibling always starts the fights or is always the one name calling, and if one sibling is always the victim, it's possible the fighting is really bullying.

Sibling rivalry is a natural part of growing up—but it can turn into bullying.

Isn't it just natural?

Parents will sometimes take an attitude that fighting between their children is just a natural part of growing up. But if what they are ignoring is really bullying, there are good reasons to pay attention.

- Children tend to continue the relationship patterns they have formed at home when they get to school. Children who bully siblings are far more likely to bully children who are their peers at school. Childhood bullying is linked to higher levels of criminal behavior in later life and academic failure. Children who are bullied by a sibling are more likely to be bullied by peers at school. Being bullied as a child is linked to emotional difficulties later in life.

- A study published in 2013 reported that being bullied by a sibling is just as damaging psychologically as being bullied by a peer.

BULLYING Q & A

Is my brother bullying me?

Q. I am two years younger than my older brother, Jay. For as long as I can remember, my older brother has terrorized me when our parents are not around. My parents feel that physical fighting between boys is natural, but my brother does things that really hurt me when our parents are away and Jay is "babysitting" me. Jay is 13 and is a lot bigger and stronger than me. When I try to tell them I am afraid of Jay, they tell me I am too sensitive. Am I being bullied? And where can I go for help?

....

A. Your parents should be taking your fears more seriously. If there is a teacher you are close to at your school, perhaps he or she would be willing to talk to your parents about your concerns. If your family belongs to a place of religious worship, such as a church or synagogue, perhaps you could talk to someone there. Or, are you in scouting? A scout master might be willing to intervene for you. If you are uncomfortable talking to anyone outside the family about your problem, perhaps you could call a hotline that specializes in bullying for advice and help, or visit a website on the topic (see pages 44-45).

You need to get help to stop your brother's bullying both for his sake and for yours. Someone in your situation is more likely to have symptoms of depression and other physical problems. Someone like your brother, who is a bully, is more likely to drop out of school or perform poorly in school, more likely to drink and smoke, and more likely to fall into juvenile delinquent behaviors. You both need to get help.

Don't Go Along With It

Bullying usually begins with small things, but it can quickly spiral out of control. If someone in your group starts bullying, you may decide that the easiest thing is to go along with it—but then you become partly responsible. On the other hand, if you are strong and make a stand against bullying, you may well be able to get it stopped.

Peer approval

Bullying behavior in a group depends on *peer approval* (approval from people your own age). Before you join in, remember how hurtful bullying is for the target.

Remember that bullies need an audience and encouragement from other peers. Without the support of onlookers, the bullying may stop. If your group starts bullying, you could have a quiet word with the ringleader, and tell him or her that this behavior is not acceptable. Studies in Canada show that in at least half of all cases, onlookers can put a stop to bullying by refusing to go along with it.

You can be strong and stand up to bullies.

BULLYING Q & A

Is this getting out of hand?

Q. The group of friends I hang out with has started bullying two younger kids on the way to school. It began with teasing, but now one of my friends has started to demand money. We all thought it was a laugh at first, but now I can see the kids are really scared. What should I do?

....

A. You're right to feel uneasy. What your friends are doing is not acceptable. Have a quiet word with them and suggest they back off before things get really out of hand. A quiet word from you might stop the bullying. If it doesn't, you should tell an adult at your school about this problem.

Is this teasing or bullying?

What Can I Do?

It can be very hard to handle group bullying if you are the target. There are many different ways to tackle the problem, and it's good to think through the options in advance. However, it's also important to judge each situation as it happens. The most important thing is to stay safe.

It's hard, but try not to react to bullying.

Ignoring bullying

One tactic is to ignore the bullies. Stay calm if possible. Shrugging and simply walking away can be a good option. If the bullies don't get a reaction, they might get bored and stop on their own. You could try to avoid places or situations in which the bullying takes place. But ignoring it may not work—some groups will carry on bullying until they are stopped.

Stand up for yourself

You may be able to stop the bullying by being assertive and saying "Stop!" or "I don't care what you say to me." Think about what you want to say in advance. You could practice in front of a mirror. Showing up the bullies in front of other people could work. Or you might try to have a private word with a group member who you think is uneasy about the bullying.

Tit for tat

Responding in kind is not the answer, whether the bullying is physical, psychological, or involves damaging property. Self-defense may be possible, but fighting back is not a good idea. If the situation gets out of hand, you could get seriously hurt or be accused of starting a fight.

Keep a record

It's always a good idea to tell a trusted adult about bullying (see pages 36-37). That adult can also help you keep a record of the bullying you are experiencing. Note down dates, times, places, and what happened. These notes may be important later on.

LONG-TERM BULLYING

Joey, now 21, comes from a mixed-race family. In primary school, he was picked on because of his skin color. Later, he was bullied because he got good grades. A text message campaign labeled him a geek. In the end, Joey told a teacher. The school confronted the bullies, and Joey got involved in a campaign to raise awareness about racism. He now campaigns against bullying in schools.

Martial arts fighters Rob McCullough and Tito Ortiz talk to students during an anti-bullying program at Huntington Beach, California.

Getting Help

If you are the target of a group of bullies, it may well be too much for you to handle on your own. Don't put yourself in danger. Tell an adult you know and trust. If the bullying is happening at school, speak to a teacher, a school counselor, or the principal about your problem. These adults are in a better position to help you by becoming involved in the situation. In addition, adults at school have the power to establish rules that make bullying at your school absolutely unacceptable.

No shame

You may feel ashamed to admit you are being bullied. But it's the bullies who should feel ashamed, not you. Remember that bullying is the cowards' way. It takes a lot of courage to speak out against a group. You may feel that the bullies will take it out on you if you tell, but schools and communities usually have ways of making sure this does not happen (see pages 40-41).

Being taken seriously

Some adults don't take bullying as seriously as they should. They may say bullying is just part of growing up or that it will help to toughen you up. If the first adult you talk to isn't sympathetic, don't give up. Think of someone else and talk to that person.

You may not always be able to handle bullying on your own.

TAKING BULLYING SERIOUSLY

Susan got involved in an acting group outside school. Four girls in the group started picking on her and calling her names. She told the director, but the director responded with, "Girls will be girls. Just ignore them." The bullying continued. In the end, Susan told her mom, who took her seriously. She and her mom discussed ways to stand up to a group of bullies. Susan was able to put these into ideas into practice, and it really helped.

Speaking Out

Everyone is affected by group bullying—not just the target and the bullies, but also bystanders, friends, and the whole school or community in which bullying is taking place. It is important to tackle bullying whenever and wherever it occurs.

Bullies need help

People who get away with bullying may well carry on with their behavior for years. It may surprise you, but bullies need help—they need help in understanding why they have started to bully. They also need to be clear that bullying is not acceptable. If the situation is allowed to continue, the bullies could be labeled as troublemakers. They could get expelled from school if the behavior is not corrected.

The school community should be a place where everyone feels safe and valued.

It's your call

If you are part of a group that starts bullying, you should speak up either to the group or to an adult about the problem. To feel good about yourself, you have to stand up for what you believe is right.

BULLYING Q & A

How do I know?

Q. I think my friend is the target of a group of bullies at my school. What should I do?

....

A. It may be hard to be sure if your friend is the target of bullies. Signs to look for include cuts and bruises, torn clothing, and damaged property. But because physical bullying is less common than other forms, also look for psychological signs, such as depression, sadness, a lack of confidence, or your friend avoiding certain social situations. Help your friend to escape any bullying situations you encounter and help him or her to talk to an adult at your school about the problem.

Schools and Bullying

Schools have a duty to stop bullying. Most schools have an anti-bullying policy, which in some schools has been developed by students as well as staff. This policy makes it clear that bullying is unacceptable, provides protection against bullying, and makes sure everyone is treated fairly.

Anti-bullying resources

Any student can ask to see the school's bullying policy or mission statement. This sets out how the school deals with bullying. Some schools have a "bullying box," which is used to anonymously report bullying.

Action to combat bullying

If you are being bullied and decide to seek help, it's a good idea to provide as much information as possible about the incidents and when and where they occurred.

The school will draw up a plan to handle the matter. They may well appoint a counselor you can talk to who will help you deal with the effects of bullying. The school might decide to move the bullies to another class, or you might be moved, if you prefer. The school may appoint another student as a buddy, to support you at times when you are at risk of bullying. If the bullying continues, the bullies could be suspended or even permanently expelled from school.

School buddies support each other against bullying.

Sharing experiences about bullying helps to raise awareness about its effects.

DEALING WITH BULLYING

Hannah was bullied by a group of girls led by Amy. Amy unjustly accused Hannah of stealing her boyfriend. The group made horrible comments about Hannah on Facebook, and sent her threatening text messages. After weeks of bullying, Hannah told a teacher, who referred her to the school counselor. The counselor talked to Amy about how the messages made her feel. She also explained to Hannah that, while we cannot control what others say about us, we can control how we think about how others treat us. When the threats got really nasty, Hannah and her counselor reported Amy to the school principal, who gave Amy a warning. When the bullying continued, Amy was eventually expelled from school.

What If I Want to Stop?

It can be hard to break with a group of bullies. Some groups will allow you to leave or to gradually spend less time with them. Others will label you a traitor. You may be scared your group will turn on you. Or, you might be surprised—there may be other people in your group who are uncomfortable with the group's bullying but afraid to speak out. You may be the one in your group to lead by example when you refuse to bully, and others in your group may follow.

Playing sports can help you let out your anger or frustration without bullying.

Help for bullies

Most schools offer support to bullies as well as targets. If you admit you have been involved in bullying, the school may provide counseling, which will help you figure out why you started bullying. The counselor may suggest ways you can manage your hurt, anger, or frustration. He or she will probably arrange a meeting with the target or targets. This can be hard, but it will help you understand the impact bullying has on others.

Avoiding labels

Some schools don't find it helpful to label "bullies" and "victims." Labeling bullying behavior, not the bullies, makes it easier for people to change the way they act.

BULLYING Q & A

Should I take action?

Q. The group of friends I hang out with has started to bully younger kids. I haven't bullied anyone, but I've seen it happen. I don't want to be disloyal. I'm also afraid my friends will turn on me. What should I do?

....

A. It's good that you did not bully these kids. However, by being a bystander and saying nothing, you are sending the message that bullying is acceptable. It's hard, but you should take action to stop the bullying. Think through the best way of tackling the situation. If you talk to your friends and they refuse to stop, you will have to report it. You may feel you are being disloyal, but in the long run you will be helping the bullies by stopping their behavior before it gets out of hand.

Help to make your school
a no bullying zone.

Additional Resources

Websites

http://www.anti-bullyingalliance.org/
  A United Kingdom-based alliance of organizations that works to stop bullying and create safer environments.

http://www.bullying.org
  A Canadian organization that provides educational programs and resources to individuals, families, educational institutions, and organizations.

http://www.bullypolice.org
  A U.S. watchdog organization advocating for bullied children and reporting on state anti-bullying laws.

http://www.cdc.gov/bam/life/index.html
  A Centers for Disease Control and Prevention (CDC) site for young adults about dealing with bullying, peer pressure, and stress.

http://www.thecoolspot.gov/pressures.asp
  A site created by the U.S. National Institute on Alcohol Abuse and Alcoholism (NIAAA) for kids 11-13 years old.

https://www.facebook.com/safety/bullying
  A campaign by Facebook and other sponsors asking everyone to show their support and spread the word against bullying. This page also has advice for people receiving abusive posts on Facebook.

http://www.glsen.org/
  A site for the Gay, Lesbian & Straight Education Network, a U.S. organization that works to create safe schools for all students, regardless of gender preference or gender identity or expression.

http://www.itgetsbetter.org/
  What began as a single YouTube video by author Dan Savage that encouraged young LGBT youth to tough it out through school, is now a website featuring thousands of videos made by youths and by celebrities attesting that life gets easier for LGBT people in adulthood.

http://www.ncpc.org/topics/bullying
  A National Crime Prevention Council website, includes a page about girls and bullying.

http://www.nobully.com
  An organization that helps schools to implement an anti-bullying program.

http://www.pacer.org/bullying/
  PACER's National Bullying Prevention Center unites, engages, and educates communities nationwide to address bullying through creative, relevant, and interactive resources. PACER's bullying prevention resources are designed to benefit all students, including students with disabilities.

http://pbskids.org/itsmylife/
  PBS advice site about issues that include family, friends, school, and emotions.

http://solutionsforbullying.com/Associations.html
  Resources for parents, teachers, and other professionals listing organizations in different countries as a starting point for getting help.

http://www.stopbullying.gov/
  A U.S. Department of Health & Human Services website with lots of information for kids, teens, parents, and educators.

http://www.violencepreventionworks.org/
  A site for the Olweus Bullying Prevention Program, an American program that has been proven to reduce bullying in schools.

Books

How to Beat Physical Bullying (Beating Bullying series) by Alexandra Handon-Harding (Rosen Central, 2013)

Bullies, Cyberbullies and Frenemies (Teen Life Confidential series) by Michelle Elliott (Wayland, 2013)

Bullying (Teen Issues series) by Lori Hile (Heinemann 2012)

Bullying Under Attack: True Stories Written by Teen Victims, Bullies & Bystanders by Stephanie Meyer, John Meyer, Emily Sperber and Heather Alexander (Health Communications, Inc., 2013)

The Bullying Workbook for Teens: Activities to Help You Deal with Social Aggression and Cyberbullying by Raychelle Cassada Lohmann and Julia V. Taylor (New Harbinger Publications, 2013)

Confessions of a Former Bully by Trudy Ludwig (Tricycle Press, 2010)

The Courage to Be Yourself: True Stories by Teens About Cliques, Conflicts, and Overcoming Peer Pressure edited by Al Desetta and Educators for Social Responsibility (Free Spirit Publishing, 2005)

The Drama Years: Real Girls Talk About Surviving Middle School – Bullies, Brands, Body Image, and More by Haley Kilpatrick and Whitney Joiner (Free Press, 2012)

Friendship Troubles (A Smart Girl's Guide series) by Patti Kelley Criswell (American Girl Publishing, revised edition, 2013)

A Guys' Guide to Conflict/A Girls' Guide to Conflict (Flip-It-Over Guides to Teen Emotions) by Jim Gallagher and Dorothy Kavanaugh (Enslow Publishers, 2008)

Hot Issues, Cool Choices: Facing Bullies, Peer Pressure, Popularity, and Put-downs by Sandra Mcleod Humphrey (Prometheus Books, 2007)

lol...OMG!: What Every Student Needs to Know About Online Reputation Management, Digital Citizenship, and Cyberbullying by Matt Ivester (Serra Knight Publishing, 2011)

Online Bullying (Teen Mental Health series) by Peter Ryan (Rosen 2012)

Peer Pressure (Issues that Concern You series) edited by Lorraine Savage (Greenhaven Press, 2009)

Peer Pressure (Tough Topics series) by Elizabeth Raum (Heinemann Library, 2008)

Physical Bullying (Take a Stand Against Bullying series) by Jennifer Rivkin (Crabtree Publishing, 2013)

Queen Bees and Wannabes by Rosalind Wiseman (Piatkus 2002; rev. edition, Three Rivers Press, 2009)

Teen Cyberbullying Investigated: Where Do Your Rights End and Consequences Begin? by Thomas A. Jacobs (Free Spirit Publishing, 2010)

Helplines (USA)

Boys Town National Hotline: 1-800-448-3000 (available to all children; toll- free)

Child-Help USA: 1-800-422-4453 (24-hour toll-free)

National Suicide Prevention Lifeline: 1-800-273-TALK (1-888-628-9454, for Spanish-speaking callers; 24-hour toll-free)

Glossary

anti-bullying policies an agreed upon set of rules or actions to stop bullying

birth order a person's age in relation to the ages of his or her siblings (for example, being the youngest or oldest child in a family); psychologists believe birth order has an effect on personality

bystander someone who watches an event but who does not intervene

cyberbullying using such information technologies as e-mail, cell phones, and instant messaging to send harmful messages

desensitized having become accustomed to hurtful behavior

direct aggression openly aggressive behavior, such as kicking, hitting, or name-calling

eating disorder an illness related to ideas and behaviors about food and body image

exclusion being deliberately left out

gay homosexual; feeling sexually attracted to a person of the same sex (gay is a term more commonly used for men than women)

gender group a set of people of the same sex

hazing initiation ceremonies that can often be dangerous and abusive in nature

homophobia a fear of, or prejudice against, people who are homosexuals

indirect aggression a kind of quiet and sneaky aggressive behavior; it could involve such actions as spreading rumors or blaming a target for something he or she did not do

isolation feeling apart from or unlike other people

lesbian a woman who is sexually attracted to women

LGBT initials that stand for lesbian, gay, bisexual, and transgender

peer pressure feeling that you should do, think, or say something because that's what others your age are doing

relational aggression a type of bullying in which the bully tries to harm the target by damaging the target's friendships or lowering the target's social status

sibling rivalry fighting, disagreements, and competition between siblings (brothers and/ or sisters)

social status how popular a person is, usually defined by the people around them

transgender a person who does not identify with the gender assigned to them at birth; for example, someone born as a male child may grow up feeling female and wear clothing and take on behaviors associated with female children

Index

Acknowledgments

Cover photo: Corbis (Serge Kozak)
Back cover photo: Shutterstock (Blaj Gabriel)

Alamy:
8-9 bottom (Bob Daemmrich), 10 (Adrian Sherratt),
14 (Angela Hampton Picture Library), 20 (John Powell
Photographer), 28 (Angela Hampton Picture Library),
33 (Ace Stock Limited), 35 (ZUMA Press, Inc.),
37 (Catchlight Visual Services).

Corbis:
4-5 (Ansgar Photography), 6 (Hero Images), 12 (Robb
D. Cohen/Retna Ltd), 17 (Odilon Dimier/PhotoAlto),
18 and 19 (ABK/BSIP), 26-27 top (Image Source),
29 (hutchinsphoto/Demotix), 30 (Rick Gomez),
32 (Ocean), 38 (Tom Grill), 41 (Brant Ward/San
Francisco Chronicle), 43 (hutchinsphoto/Demotix).

Shutterstock:
7 (Pressmaster), 8-9 top (Tracy Whiteside),
11 (Monkey Business Images), 13 (Tyler Olson),
15 (CREATISTA), 16 (Carlos E. Santa Maria),
21 (Petrenko Andriy), 22 (CREATISTA), 23 (Golden
Pixels LLC), 24 (Chepko Danil Vitalevich), 25 (Jochen
Schoenfeld), 26-27 bottom (Jacek Chabraszewski),
31 (Greenland), 34 (CREATISTA), 36 (Monkey Business
Images), 39 (Andrey Shadrin), 40 (Lisa F. Young),
42 (Lorraine Swanson).